Oscar Schwartz | the honeymoon stage

New Poems

GIRAMONDO POETS

Oscar Schwartz | the honeymoon stage

First published 2017
from the Writing & Society Research Centre
at Western Sydney University
by the Giramondo Publishing Company
PO Box 752 Artarmon NSW 1570 Australia
www.giramondopublishing.com

Designed by Harry Williamson
Typeset by Andrew Davies
in 10/16.5 pt Baskerville BT

Printed and bound by Ligare
Distributed in Australia by NewSouth Books

National Library of Australia
Cataloguing-in-Publication data:

Schwartz, Oscar –
the honeymoon stage / Oscar Schwartz
ISBN 978-1-925336-39-9 (pbk)
A821.4

The I, You and We in these pages do not belong to me, but came into being inside the boundless, invisible space in which we now spend much of our time.

Contents

part two

you

the honeymoon stage

i

good news about the future
everyone is married to everyone
therefore you are married to someone you love
but according to logic you are
also married to someone you hate
to people you have never met, to your family
to every politician in the world, you are also married to
    celebrities
and to use logic once more, even if you don't love me now
trust me, we are married in the future

ii

what of our inevitable honeymoon?
i have made a reservation in fiji, a four star resort
with a good seafood buffet
complimentary massage and sulfur baths
you will become so comfortable that
you'll have to go snorkelling three times a day to stay awake
your body will become soft with tropical sea water
you will love snorkelling, it will drive you insane

part one
us

lance armstrong

i

yesterday lance armstrong admitted to being a drug cheat
today i found a lance armstrong bracelet in a bird's nest
that had fallen from a tree outside a church
is it a sign i should take seriously
does it mean that you want us to get back together?

ii

i found this today in a bird's nest outside a church
i don't know what it means
it reminded me of you
how i am so excited by you
how you make me feel even better than when i feel
    fashionable
how nothing could improve your looks
i thought maybe you left it there for me
either way
will you accept this lance armstrong bracelet?

beautiful imperfect machines

it was raining when i saw the beautiful machine
wait i didn't really see a beautiful machine
but i imagined that i saw a beautiful machine
and it was really raining
and while i only imagined it
i sincerely wanted to tell you about it
but i couldn't do it in english
because the machine was too beautiful for english
so i invented a language
a grammar and an entire vocabulary
and without warning i was practising it at night
in front of the mirror, becoming fluent
i start teaching it to you
and we spend half an hour every night speaking it
you become fluent, construct sophisticated sentences
you speak better than me
you correct my mistakes in grammar and syntax
on weekends we go for long walks and talk the language
we are so engrossed in it that we forget where we're walking
and have to use our phones to get home
we don't speak english anymore
we stop going out to see friends
at the shops we speak broken english
we develop strange accents
people think we are from a foreign country
one night in spring when it is raining

and we are walking in the city
i finally describe to you the beautiful machine i saw
and you start crying
and i say “it’s a beautiful machine isn’t it?”
you say “no it’s a beautiful language”
and i say “no it’s a beautiful machine”
and you say “no, shut up, let’s just enjoy the rain”

ellen degeneres

if there is one thing you know without doubt
it is the pleasure of arabica coffee beans
if there is one thing you do with abandon
it is an above average irish accent
we consider these facts in the kitchen
and i encourage you to apply to the ellen degeneres show
to perform your irish accent, to which you respond
"let's say i do apply and i do make it on the show
ellen will ask me to dance before my segment and
if there is one thing i promised myself i would never do
it is dance on cable television"
i look at you in the kitchen drinking coffee
if i know one thing about you it is that
even if you did get on the ellen degeneres show
you would not be changed by your sudden fame
you would come home and talk of the pleasure
of arabica coffee beans and for this alone you
remain more reliable than caffeine
more true than the latest season of the
endlessly popular ellen degeneres show

what side of the bed does your clone sleep on?

i had a bad dream my clone says what was it you say
and roll over to my clone's side of the bed and put your
hand on its bicep my clone begins to tell you about the
bad dream you half listen and put your lips to its chest
are you even listening my clone says kind of you reply

at this moment i walk into the bedroom and i see you
with your lips on my clones chest i made breakfast i say
i boiled some eggs

i had a bad dream my clone says oh yeah what was it
about i reply come back to bed and i'll tell you about it
but i'm already dressed it's nice and warm in here my
clone says while patting the mattress with its hand

i get back into bed with you and my clone i am wearing
black jeans and a polar fleece you are in pink pyjamas
and my clone is naked i am in the middle of you and
my clone it is warm i fall into a light sleep

i wake up and you are gone it's just me and my clone
in bed together what time is it i ask and then realise
that i'm naked and that my clone is wearing your pink
pyjamas relax my clone says

i reach for my phone its 9.12am where did she go i ask
she's at work my clone replies you should be at work
i say why do you do this every morning my clone says

i turn away from my clone and read emails on my
phone there is one email from you it is about our
dinner plans i feel my clone touch my back with its
lips i'm sorry for shouting at you my clone says i didn't
sleep well last night i'm nervous and i feel a bit sick

i put down my phone and turn to give my clone a hug
but i find that my clone is out of bed now fully dressed
in black jeans and a polar fleece what do you want for
breakfast my clone asks i'm boiling eggs if you want

but now i feel cold and tired i pull the sheets up to my
eyes don't worry about me i say i think i'm going to stay
in bed for a bit longer my clone sighs and closes the
door i fall back asleep and have a dream

you are the species in my head

my thoughts about you
are a species with an evolutionary history
and a developed culture
my thoughts about you
communicate with each other through language
my thoughts about you write each other novels
my thoughts about you sometimes
feel like an aggressive imperialistic species
that has plans to conquer and destroy
all my other thoughts
and then my brain
and then my cheeks and lips
and finally my tongue

today you asked me if i remember what you told me about love

i said
no i don't remember
i was lying
i do remember
you were sitting in a bamboo armchair wearing bike shorts
i don't know why i pretended i didn't remember
surely now after so much time i should be relaxed around you
i lied to you
i'm sorry
it's just that what you said about love reminded me
of the worthlessness of things
someone once told me that someone i dislike has a small dick
it made me feel better
which i know is stupid and immature
the reasons i dislike him are also immature
but they're not stupid
they're fine

a picture at a party

we get dressed in your sister's room
we walk up the middle of a road to a party
we walk in together but shortly after
i can't find you
but then i find you in the kitchen
talking to two people
one is wearing medieval armour
the other is wearing a pikachu onesie
i say something to you
you say something to pikachu
the person wearing medieval armour laughs
pikachu says something to me
you'll have to speak up i say
you laugh
this continues for some time
until medieval armour person
takes out a phone
and arranges us in a certain way
and takes a picture
we look at the picture together
you look so cute you say to pikachu
i leave the party

the death of the melbourne shuffle

you are as important to me as the melbourne shuffle
that grew inside the clubs of the 1990s
you are like my 1990s in the sense
that you provide a personal history of things
do you remember that time in the club
when a short guy had talcum powder in his pocket
and he sprinkled it on the ground
and made everyone stand in a circle around him
and then slid his feet to the music
why did he do that
was that the death of the melbourne shuffle

i've seen you in my dreams of the 1990s
i've seen you dance in the clubs of melbourne
you do most of your movement with your arms
it's your personal style
but it will never move beyond the personal
towards something timeless and
potentially marketable

i sat on lungs

when i visited your family for the first time i brought
my own chair to sit on and everything was going great
and your family was really happy but in the middle
of all that happiness i realised that the chair i brought
was actually a pair of lungs

i looked down and saw how pink the lungs were and
i could feel their laboured respiration and everyone
could hear them almost asthmatic under my weight
and unexpectedly you started crying for the giant
prehistoric animal who gave up its lungs for me
to sit on

your family comprised of vegetarians looked at me
disapprovingly and i excused myself and pulled the
lungs out the front door towards the train station at
which point they shrunk to the size of a teddy bear so
i held them on my lap and boarded the train

the other people on the train were breathless and
eyeing the lungs so i cupped the lungs which were
now the same size as my wallet in my hand and with
the other i petted them using the outside of my
forefinger very gently almost imperceptibly tickling
the minuscule alveoli

i arrived home without any missed calls from you so i placed the lungs which were now a regular human size on a chair opposite me i feel terrible i told the lungs and the lungs encouraged me to write about my day do it calmly the lungs said do it breathlessly just be quiet stop breathing let me do that for you

your new diet

i met you just after you started a new diet
every day you would eat only that which was related to a
    food memory
sometimes you would tell me the story behind your diet
for example there was the day you ate a box of
    freddo frogs
and you told me that it was a reminder of the time you
    stole a box of
freddo frogs from the school cafeteria
and ate them one by one on the school bus home
other times it was easy for me to guess the memory
for example there was the time i came home and
    the apartment looked
like a 10 year old's birthday and we ate rainbow cake
    for dinner
you also ate things that you didn't distinctly remember
but that your parents told you they had fed you
like sweet potato mash or fish boiled in milk
i learnt a lot about your childhood by watching you eat
lots of pasta, mangoes, almonds, not much meat
we also went to quite a few average suburban restaurants
many of them had changed cuisine or ownership since
    you were a child
but we'd eat there anyway, which made no sense to me
mostly the new diet was healthy and conservative
but on the days when your memories

led you back to what you had once desired
the eating could become extreme and manic
there were times when you became secretive about
    your memories
like the day you cut up the pillow cases
into tiny pieces and swallowed them
when i asked what memory you had of eating pillow cases
    you replied
what do you care? this new diet is doing wonders
i look and i feel fantastic i bounce right out of bed

untitled

it felt like it was made out of bodies
but really it was made out of language
illuminated in white fluorescent letters on a scoreboard
that kept a record of the words we used
the private language that accumulated between us
like a small goldfish in a plastic bag
left on a park bench
that accidentally rolled into the sewer
and drifted out to sea
a bag of fresh water and a fish in it
surrounded by an ocean
until the plastic gave way
and the fish escaped
and used its muscles to inhale through its gills
trying desperately to filter oxygen out of the salty water
eventually dying of a tiny heart attack
and all the while
making adorable splashing noises

kanye west's song runaway

while on a bus filled with the faces of people trying to sleep
some of them with their mouths open
some with smiles suggesting good dreams
some scared due to driving down a mountain
at night in heavy snow
me and you are listening to kanye west's song
        runaway
sharing headphones
one in each ear

towards the end of the song
kanye starts screaming
his voice is distorted beyond comprehension
after a few minutes it sounds like he's crying
i nudge you with my elbow
you're sitting in the window seat
you pull your head up off the glass

how good is this song i say
i can't hear the lyrics you say
i think that's the point i say
no i mean my headphone is broken

part two
you

how you woke up and thought everyone had been
replaced by automated versions of themselves

how you decided to stop intervening in your own life

how you thought security guards with machine
guns were standing outside storehouses in a desert
somewhere

and how those desert storehouses were filled with inner
peace

how you told me that when i didn't sleep over you
would use a giant slice of white bread as a pillow

how you wore your most colourful outfits in pitch black
rooms

how you imagined lab rats floating towards freedom on
life rafts

how you thought that the old lady's arm was disfigured
but it wasn't she was just holding a baguette

how you always chose amphetamines

how when you finally slept you slept like a can of tuna
that was swallowed by a blue whale

how you said it felt like reality was taking drugs to
escape you

how you often had conversations with yourself in which
you would pretend to be competent at things like
accounting

how you said you wanted to build a career that relied on a single, tenuous, inane gimmick, which was constantly at risk of getting old

how hard you prayed for invading aliens

how you looked for inner peace in other people

how you treated your friends objectively like skyscrapers

and how your sincerity was a technique

how you pictured your dad and mum living in the jungle and smiling

and how, after waking, you always felt certain you had been kidnapped

how, for you, the easy things were hard and the hard things were also hard how badly you wanted to be a better person, an impossibly better person

how your voice was like a text for which i felt a detached, objective pleasure yet whose provenance was, by definition, unknowable

how when you cried you sounded like a moth trying dutifully to be graceless and forget its vocabulary

how you reminded me that before fire there was body warmth

how every night i fell asleep and woke up the main
character stuck in your landscape like a clumsy
organic monster

how you wanted to fill a room with fish hooks hanging
from the roof and chase me through it

how you wrote on my dad's facebook wall "george bush
sucks nietszche's dick"

how you were constantly trying to convince me that
you were human

how something about you reminded me of a buffet
on death row

how you reminded me more of the large pip in
an avocado than the small pips on the outside of
strawberries

how when you hugged me i felt like i was submerged
in a warm body of water which was somehow conscious
and massaging me

how you kept pointing to bodies of water that i couldn't
see or comprehend

how sometimes when i was with you it felt like you were
floating miles out in the ocean in a storm surrounded
by countless pieces of historically significant priceless art

how when you were doing something you wanted
me to watch you doing it from a distance and not do
anything else

how the world feels immense compared with one
week ago

how love felt like the opposite of practice

the world's youngest desert

in a young desert
one of the youngest on the planet
where the sand is still clean and the dunes
mountainous the camels infantile and adorable
there is an inbox and in this inbox
there is spam
the spam tells of anti-ageing medication
of botox and silicone and it is
written by hand in the cursive script
of your mother, bold and legible
just like the permission slips
she would sign and leave
by the door for your sisters
so they wouldn't have to compete
in the swimming carnivals at school

language giving birth to itself in our mouths

your name is xyz
you have been accused of a terrible crime
you have to go into hiding and take on a pseudonym
from now on i will refer to you as sarah
sarah, you are not alone in this
because in the future most of us will be forced to
    use pseudonyms
in the second future no one will know their real name
children will be born and given a pseudonym
pets will be given pseudonyms
abstract nouns will be given pseudonyms
it is possible that by the third future we will call
    'happiness' 'rebecca'
and we will call 'rebecca' 'seaweed'
in the fourth future the giving of pseudonyms will be
    non uniform
meaning that in the fifth future we will be endlessly confused
and in the sixth future we will talk aimlessly
hoping to be understood by coincidence
so that by the seventh future we will talk with no meaning
like poets and we will be living in caves too
but then for some unknown reason the eighth future
    will happen
and everyone will be free
and we will come out into the sunlight
and start swapping our names back

i can imagine it now
you will walk up to a beautiful man and you will know
  straight away
you will say to him you look like someone called sarah
and he will say to you, you look like someone called xyz
and you will embrace for a minute then shake hands
and in the ninth future you will swap your names back
everyone will start swapping their names back
and this action will be repeated over and over
and we will authenticate each other
so that by the tenth future
we will once again feel language giving birth to itself in
  our mouths

honestly how could you have known

if you cut open an avocado
and found instead of a pip
me naked and bald
skin slightly green
and you put the two halves
back together and
wrapped the broken avocado
in a towel and
buried it in the garden
in the hope that i would
grow into something larger
more human and less pip
who could blame you for that?

how could you have known?
that if instead you had pried me out
cleaned me
let me eat the green flesh
from which i was born
i would've become
not only your lifelong friend
but a money-maker
happily making appearances
on talk shows happy to be
famous for my smallness
and unusual inhuman origins

happy to oblige the cameras
with small daring acts
like having to compete against mice
in a mock olympics

god will send you nudes

if you've been feeling guilty
about all the sinful things
you've been enjoying on the internet
try to seek consolation
in the presence of your ancestors

in time, god will send you nudes

the first 15 minutes of a science fiction movie

you arrive in a new suburb on a saturday afternoon
the people are gathered at the football ground
where the local team is playing
at half time you start telling people that you are
artificial intelligence escaped from the lab
a few of the mothers listen to your story
while they lean on a balustrade
but when the second half starts they tell you to be quiet

the local team wins the football match
in the team rooms after the game
everyone is huddled in a circle
you push your way into the middle of the room
and say in a loud voice
"i am artificial intelligence escaped from the lab"
the footballers, who are an average age of sixteen, laugh
they ruffle your hair and slap you on the back
it is at this precise moment that you begin
to plot the downfall of the human race

you forgot your mother's face

in the presence of a photo of
your mother, aged twenty three
her hands folded and covered in glitter
her hair long and black
sitting with young men in mcdonalds
whose faces, next to hers
appear handsome and directionless
her mouth open and heart shaped
it suddenly dawns on you
that as the glitter comes to rest,
as it predictably does, as it always does,
on our eyelids, setting
us on fire with the glamour of the past
you suddenly forget her perfection and
in time you forget your mother's face

you were only six at the time

after six years of life
you went to a michael jackson concert with your dad
who was wearing a silver leather jacket

you were wearing a skirt with butterflies
he told you to stand on his shoulders to see better
when michael jackson moonwalked
you felt all the butterflies on your skirt
turn into razor blades

michael jackson threw his towel into the crowd
a woman caught it and put it to her face
remember

what appears to be an australian memory

you're having the same conversation
we had years ago
your weekends are wrapped in our last words
were we always travelling parallel to the sea
were the mountains always on our left
you tell me you're in the city now
you often go shopping at the supermarket
and open packets of golden cookies
you have boys staying at your house
you cook them dinner
you drive them into the hills to meet your mother
who reminds them to tuck their shirts in
which reminds you of my uniform
ripped up and tossed in the river
you call my name twice and then you're silent
you make collages of us in the garage
you don't know what you did
but you feel like you shouldn't have done it
you're in bed early
you think you can hear an owl in your bedroom
on your pillow
you don't open your eyes
this is all much harder than it sounds

late at night in the gym what do you look like?

precisely like someone who is using a treadmill
wearing grey shorts, an extremely grey singlet
walking (not jogging, not running)
at a constant speed of six kilometers per hour
at an incline of three
and your face is expressionless to the extent that
you don't look like a person because
you look like a machine
that has been engineered
to move its legs unremittingly (not rhythmically,
    without strain)
but mechanically
and the treadmill you're walking on
looks like a person
that is using you for exercise
rolling its fleshy conveyor belt underneath your feet
until it becomes exhausted
and rolls from underneath you
and leaves the gym
but forgets to turn you off
so you stay there

hovering one foot above the ground
legs dangling and rotating
hands clutching an invisible hand rest
eyes immoveable on the tv screen opposite you
which has been turned off
which is now a black mirror
in which you can see a reflection

self help book

at 2am you discover that
you are the last edible thing on earth
and as you begin to eat
before every bite
the mouth takes pause to thank the body
and the body sweats in anticipation

pet weasel

when your pet weasel died around one week ago
you threw its body into a street-side rubbish bin
and you cleaned out the cage with disinfectant
soon after a friend from school came over to watch a movie
you were sitting together in your room
“i wonder if i could fit in that cage?” the friend said
“you should try” you replied
the friend was small and flexible and managed
to squeeze in
you both laughed
you closed the latch to the cage and
you both laughed some more
a few moments went by
your friend stopped laughing
“ok you can let me out now” your friend said

10 best dunks of michael jordan

if you're worried about your parents
dying think about tourism think about
horses think about mushrooms
and flowers in storm water gutters
think about the productivity of
the internet and compare it with
the presence of tulips
think of something fluorescent
attach it to something muscular
and conceive of the ten best dunks
of michael jordan

how to write an e book of poetry

be part of the unchanging collection of mass and energy in the universe

become manifest as a tiny foetus created out of the unchanging collection of mass and energy through the process of your parents having sex

get born

spend approximately 12 years vaguely experiencing things

spend approximately 4 years becoming aware of experiences

become self aware

start reading

spend time reading

feel for the first time a sense of not being part of the unchanging collection of mass and energy in the universe and slowly contemplate how this feeling is like what you've read about, that you are experiencing loneliness for the first time

feel lonely

spend time alone

find a book that allows you to dissociate fully from past conceptions of yourself

read that book many times

carry the book with you everywhere

buy a backpack

put the book in the backpack

try to become a character in the book

try to become the writer of the book

try to write exactly the same book but in your own voice and fail

feel frustrated and worthless

feel doubt

feel inconsolable doubt one night in particular

go for a walk

suddenly realise that you have confused your ability to read and enjoy or appreciate a book with your ability to write

make some money doing a job

start writing

slowly realise that you might be able to write something

join the internet

see many people writing

make a tumblr devoted to the books you read

gain 24 notes on a review of a book in which you compare reading the book to sipping on a can of diet coca cola

feel confident

feel funny

feel intelligent

feel a sense of entitlement

spend full days in front of the internet

feel part of the ever-changing collection of information on your screen

get rejected by literary journals

make a blog post about how many times you have been rejected by literary journals

get 12 notes

feel depressed

feel jealous

feel inadequate

feel doubt and fear that you have come nowhere since you started writing

reach out to people on the internet

make an internet friend called elise

tell elise about your grandparents

read elise's emails about her earliest memories

travel to where elise lives to meet her

have lunch with elise

spend 3 months doing things with elise

spend 1 day alone when elise returns to university

spend 1 afternoon messaging elise while she is at university

feel insecure

spend 1 night awake while elise lies next to you and decide you do not

want to feel insecure

leave elise and go to your parents house

live with your parents for 3 weeks

go away for the weekend with old friends

return to the city

find an apartment

start a new tumblr

start writing about your experiences on the internet

start using the language of the internet to write

write a poem about twitter and use words like 'irl' in a way that is sincere in the sense that you use the word 'irl' all the time but also slightly ironic in that 'poetry' is supposed to be a place where internet acronyms are not allowed

feel freed from convention

hand write a poem about the internet

read it 14 times in one day

decide that it is the best thing you've ever written, that everything else has lead up to this point, that it would be a good idea to delete all other poems you've ever written

delete old poems off hard drive

start writing a handwritten poem about the internet every day for 72 days

read them to your sister

laugh insecurely when your sister isn't amazed by your poems and you say yeh maybe they're not that good but secretly think that your sister doesn't spend enough time on the internet and couldn't understand them

start taking pictures of your 72 handwritten internet poems and posting them online

start getting followers

get 215 new followers

get featured on #poetry on tumblr

receive 140000 notes in 24 hours

type up your 72 handwritten internet poems

get a friend from high school who has since become a successful graphic

designer to help you lay the poems out in a design that is easily readable

collate the newly designed poems into a pdf and give it a title

the title should be '72 handwritten internet poems'

start sending the pdf to various small press publishers

start an excel spreadsheet that documents all the places you send your pdf get 34 rejections

get an email while sitting on the toilet in a bar while drunk that says your

pdf has been accepted by a publisher of online e books

be happy and relieved

read the email another two times

flush the toilet

tell your friends

promote your e book online

get interviewed by a few small literary blogs

get a girlfriend

start calling your girlfriend your partner

feel happy

feel good

feel anxious

feel dissatisfied

go for a walk one night and panic when you see a broken chessboard on the sidewalk

become obsessed with the fact a pawn in the game of
chess doesn't have to move in the way it does, that it
could move in any direction, that it could be replaced

with any other material or shape, and that language
and word s are exactly the same and that your poems,
your writing, are meaningless

watch your partner's disinterest in your existential crisis

watch you ruin your relationship

travel

come home

train to become a nurse

become a nurse

start working as a nurse in a hospital

feel good and part of the unchanging pile of mass and
energy pulsating through the universe

die

get buried

decompose

become diffuse among various organic materials
on earth

be there as a collection of diffuse organic materials
when humanity ends

be there as a collection of diffuse organic materials
when planet earth ends

explode outwards into space with planet earth

become diffuse among the various chemicals in
the universe

become more and more dispersed

undergo unknowable transformations over
unknowable lengths of time

for a brief time become part of the consciousness of
some super intelligent life form

observe that all previous intelligent data on earth has
been accumulated by this super intelligent life force

view your e book of poetry again amidst the troves
of intelligent data

be there when the super intelligent life form
disintegrates for a reason beyond your comprehension

become diffuse consciousness in the universe

become reduced entirely to hydrogen atoms floating
billions of light years away from each other

spend many eternities doing unknown things

start vibrating rapidly

become infinitely fast and infinitely hot

end in a way that is, by definition, unknowable

wow she says cool sky

woke up and in front of the sky there was a small
satellite dish stuck to a building i got out of bed and
walked towards my phone touched my phone and took
it back into bed i pressed on two things

the first thing spoke of the delusion of twenty five year
olds of the simultaneous existence of coconut water
and climate change the second thing was written by
a nasa scientist who spoke of a crumbling civilisation
of a growing gap between elites and the rest how
it happened to the romans how it happened to the
mayans how it will happen to us who is us i thought
lying on my side holding my phone what is civilisation

i got out of bed and did body weight exercises had
a shower muesli a conversation with my housemate
who just read a study that proves that meat proteins
are bad for humans i fed the fish drank coffee drove
to university along a freeway observed trucks driving
in a row the sky was pale blue with some white on
the horizon

in the afternoon my sister called to say she couldn't come to see a play with me because she is pregnant and the play is about frankenstein i am crying at kleenex ads on tv she said that's ok i understand i said i am due to have a baby in four weeks she said i know i said

in the evening i ate curry i paid and walked homewards through the busy street then turned around and went back to the restaurant to buy a mango lassi

now i'm in my room sitting next to the window the guy in the apartment above me had an operation on his sinuses and has not left his room for a week he is twenty eight i see his girlfriend in the garage of our apartment sitting on the floor smoking a cigarette using a small japanese glass with a cartoon elephant on it as an ashtray she is twenty six i hear footsteps on the floorboards above me look at the sky he says to his girlfriend out of the window jesus would you look at the sky his twenty six year old girlfriend lifts up her head wow she says cool sky

in the club part one

i'm not addicted to pills
i just love the smell
like autumn leaves
i would crush them up
and smell them
like the sun
or like rihanna
i would
love it if she sang
a cover of 'hot stuff'
by donna summer
'hot stuff baby this evening'
she'd sing
and her eyes would fill
with tears of pure diet
pepsi
like she had been staring
at the sun
dreaming of barbados in
the fall or like she had walked
into a room
and smelled the leaves
for the first time
and was dazzled
finally in love

in the club part two

a story about
someone else's life took
off and became a self help
book after that it became
a nightclub
besides i worry that i'm starting
to sound like the club and
the club sounds like a python hissing
some seductive code
i'd like to remain idle like goethe
(who is goethe?)
or the clouds
as they molest
each other over the d floor
i'd like to offer the club a little possum
with pink eyes that dances
how many pills do i owe you what are my
limits again will i find new ones
in some ridiculous gesture like
a death stare or does it exist
on a bike pedalling out into
the ocean with no limit in sight besides
a lens with its magnetic finger
pointed straight at you

should i watch game of thrones?

will i be entertained?

will the rest of the world become irrelevant

will it provide a distraction from my life

is that what most people want from tv

is that what most people want from art

will watching it make me want to write a think piece about art and life?

will i write a think piece in which i contend that game of thrones is somehow a reflection of some broader aesthetic issue?

will i start a blog dedicated to exploring how this broader aesthetic issue plays itself out in game of thrones?

will this blog bring me notoriety?

will it make me momentarily controversial, so controversial that i stop writing on the internet and stop watching game of thrones?

or will i stop watching game of thrones for another unrelated reason? will my reason be that i just don't have time anymore because i started indoor rock climbing?

or will my reason be that you suddenly stopped being part of my life and i feel uncomfortable watching it without you?

will game of thrones always remind me of you?

when the game of thrones movie comes out in a few
years will i ring you for the first time in ages?

will i say: would you like to see game of thrones movie
for old times sake?

will you say yes?

if you do say yes and we go to see game of thrones
movie, will we think the movie was good?

will we discuss its strengths and weaknesses after while
eating ice cream?

will you sarcastically refer to the movie as a box office
hit?

will i laugh at your sarcasm?

will i feel ok when the night ends and you go one way and i go another?

will i go home and look up facts about the movie game of thrones?

will i learn that game of thrones movie grossed a record breaking amount of money at the box office?

will i message you this information?

will you message back?

will a few aimless months go by after you don't message me back?

wait i have a few more questions about game of thrones

like should i watch game of thrones on a tv or on my computer?

should i buy it or stream it or download it illegally? if i download it illegally will i get caught?

if i get caught will i be fined?

will i be the first person in australia fined by an american media company for illegally downloading game of thrones?

will this be what i become notorious for?

will my court case for pirating game of thrones inspire me to get a degree in law and fight for changes in copyright?

will it make me an advocate for new intellectual property rights?

will i start a blog about the ever-changing landscape of digital media or will it make me meek and scared?

will the media attention force me to retreat inwards?

will i be too scared to leave the house due to the media circus surrounding my illegal downloading activities?

will i sit inside and watch reruns of game of thrones?

will game of thrones be all i have left?

will i blame game of thrones for my downfall?

or will i blame you?

that is to say: will i blame myself or will i blame the world?

will i start dressing like characters from game of thrones while alone in my room?

does my physique suit game of thrones attire?

if so will i become bold enough to leave my house
wearing game of thrones attire?

will you love me if i dress like game of thrones
characters? will you think i'm eccentric?

will you think i'm being my authentic self?

or will you think that i'm a slave to whatever's new?

essentially a person without a centre

a hollow, scare-crowed person

someone who latches on to trends

regurgitates them

achieves moderate notoriety doing so but then becomes scared by the notoriety

can't handle the criticism

retreats inwards

waits until criticism stops

and then repeats the whole process again

wait i have a few more questions about game of thrones

do any of the characters in game of thrones fall in love with each other?

do any of the actors that play the characters date in real life?

does their offscreen romance increase the tension of their onscreen romance?

has the narrative of the show infected their perception of one another?

when the show ends will they have nothing left to say to each other?

will they be sitting opposite one another one night in beverly hills and realise that they fell in love with a narrative and not with a person?

will they leave each other and fall in love with a new co star?

or will they move to a small house in the country and pretend they are still living game of thrones?

will they buy life-sized mannequins and dress them up
as the full cast of game of thrones?

and go hunting for food?

and throw lavish banquets for the mannequins?

would this be a good thing for them to do?

would it be a distraction from life?

would it be delusional?

are delusions what get us through?

is game of thrones the ultimate delusion?

is game of thrones the grand delusion i've been
waiting for?

a fuckable robot

paint for me
an alluring robot covered in fur
a naked robot drenched in oil
flanked by muscular robots holding spices
and buckets of gold
sexy robots dripping in diamonds
drenched in perfume
exotic robots in dim light and the faint waft of rare incense
a demure robot in a white bonnet
a sultry robot bathing in hot springs
a horny robot
a romantic robot reading by candlelight
a tragic robot sailing off into the golden horizon
a heroic robot riding a brown horse
an unattainable robot by the windowsill
a mysterious robot veiled by peacock feathers
a robot holding a pick axe with bulging forearms
a robot in pearls
a robot in a velvet ball gown
a naked robot swimming in a champagne bath
an athletic robot holding a helmet
a robot with a narrow waist
an oil painting of a fuckable robot
painted on tight fresh robot canvass

please skip to the last line of this poem and read from the bottom up

and pretend this never happened
but once you reach the end you can start reading top down
now you are welcome to keep reading
did that reduce your boredom briefly?
until he gets into bed and does some things i don't know
and imagines giving himself a highly processed dog treat
and he gives his dog a highly processed treat
something about her hair
when his sister was still alive and they were on a beach
and then when he was only 6
when he was 20
and remembers some things about when he was 30
while he washes up the dishes
which he pats once every 5 minutes or so
and a mini schnauzer
will there be incense
and eat with his legs crossed on a pillow
will he cook
is he alone?
does he think carefully about what he has for dinner
does he care about food
does he drink tea
does he shower when he gets home
considering the traffic
listening to the radio

driving home from work
if you're bored maybe you might like to imagine a british male
are you bored, he asks
the title is the whole point of this poem
wait, he says
he is wearing a denim jacket
he is bald and has a dyed blonde goatee
now imagine a 65 year old british male
never to speak again
and so by this line the lovers have already left each other
feels that the other is a blind conformist
yet the person who read from the top down
feels that the other is by nature inconsiderate
because the person who read from the bottom up
but then there is an insurmountable tension between them
they will meet here in this line and fall in love
the other from the top down
one from the bottom up
there are two people reading this poem

Acknowledgements

Some of the poems in this collection have previously appeared in *Australian Book Review, The Age, The Lifted Brow, Spork Press* and *Rabbit*.

The Giramondo Publishing Company acknowledges the support of Western Sydney University in the implementation of its book publishing program.